GAME, SET, SISTERS!

The Story of Venus and Serena Williams

Jay Leslie ✦ Illustrated by **Ebony Glenn**

A WHO DID IT FIRST? BOOK

HENRY HOLT AND COMPANY

NEW YORK

On a crumbling court in Compton,
five sisters dodged. They dove. They pumped
their fists as they shouted the score.

The Williams sisters were inseparable—all five of them. Every morning, Yetunde, Isha, Lyndrea, Venus, and little Serena piled into a dirty yellow Volkswagen that coughed and clanked its way to the tennis court.

Under their father's watchful eye, they played, serving and sprinting and lunging and laughing, swinging racquets that were bigger than they were.

Tennis let them all be together.

At the end of each day, they collapsed into bed, so sweaty that the sheets stuck to their skin.

Serena often crawled into Venus's bed and fell asleep with her head on her big sister's shoulder.

"I'm going to be the best in the world one day," Serena whispered sleepily.

Venus grinned at her. "You'll have to go through me first, Meeka," she said.

One by one, the older Williams sisters set down their racquets until only Venus and Serena were left.

Because they didn't belong to cushy country clubs or have world-class coaches, they had to be creative about their training. They did whatever it took to have the **strongest arms**,

the **fastest feet,**

the **smartest strategy,**

and the **most graceful moves.**

Soon, Venus and Serena were ready to play in tournaments.
They knew they would have to face off eventually—but they
didn't expect it to happen in their very first tournament together!
Venus and Serena found themselves head-to-head in the finals.

POW!
Venus served.

BAM!
Serena returned.

THWACK!
Venus struck.

BLAM!
Serena swung with all her might.

But . . . she missed.

Venus won. She grinned for the camera—but then
she noticed her sister sitting quietly on the sidelines.

"Hey, Serena," Venus said when they got home. "Let's switch trophies. I like the silver one better anyway."

"Really?" asked Serena, eyes wide.

Venus nodded.

Serena held the gold trophy in her arms.

Then she held her sister tighter.

Unfortunately, the Williams sisters were about to be split up. Venus and Serena had learned everything they could in Compton, California. They needed to move to Florida to attend an elite tennis academy if they wanted to keep getting better.

Once they got there, one thing became obvious: Venus was going to be the best in the world.

Spectators told her father, "You have a legend on your hands."

Every time someone complimented Venus, Serena turned red. "What about me?"

Venus knew that her sister also had greatness in her.

"Don't try to play like me, Serena," she said. "You have to play like yourself."

Serena took her big sister's advice, and the two got better and better and better.

Venus turned pro in 1994 when she was just fourteen years old.

Serena followed close on her sister's heels one year later.

They began winning tournaments worldwide.

They crushed the competition in Chicago.

They mopped up their opponents in Moscow.

They played powerfully in Paris.

And soon their names were on everyone's lips.

But despite all of their trophies and success, the sisters
faced challenges on the court . . . and off.

They were two of the strongest and most successful
athletes in the world, but they were also Black.

Journalists sometimes referred to them as gorillas, and their wealthy white competitors accused them of cheating—there was no way two Black girls from Compton could be this good at tennis!

But the sisters ignored them, focusing on giving every match their all.

In one of their favorite tournaments, Venus had to withdraw because of an injury.

Serena hugged her sister tight and said, "I'll play hard enough for the both of us!" She raced out, ready to win.

But as soon as she stepped onto the court, the crowd erupted into jeers and boos. They screamed terrible, racist things at both sisters and their dad.

Even after she won, Serena broke down in tears,
shaking in anger and pain.

"I'm never coming back here," Serena said.

"Then neither am I," said Venus.

As always, the girls stood together and fought together . . .
and won together. Venus and Serena were soon on top
of the world.

But that world was about to come crashing down.

Their big sister Yetunde was shot and killed in Compton,
near the crumbling courts where they all used to play.

Four sisters—Isha, Lyndrea, Venus, and Serena—
gathered in California to be together.

"It's okay to cry," said Venus, but Serena couldn't.

Crying would make Yetunde's death real.

Venus was heartbroken, and seeing her little sister in so much pain made her feel worse. She'd always been the role model, the leader, the protector. She'd always known what to do.

But now she felt powerless.

The next few years were the most difficult they had ever faced. Venus and Serena, once inseparable, drifted apart.

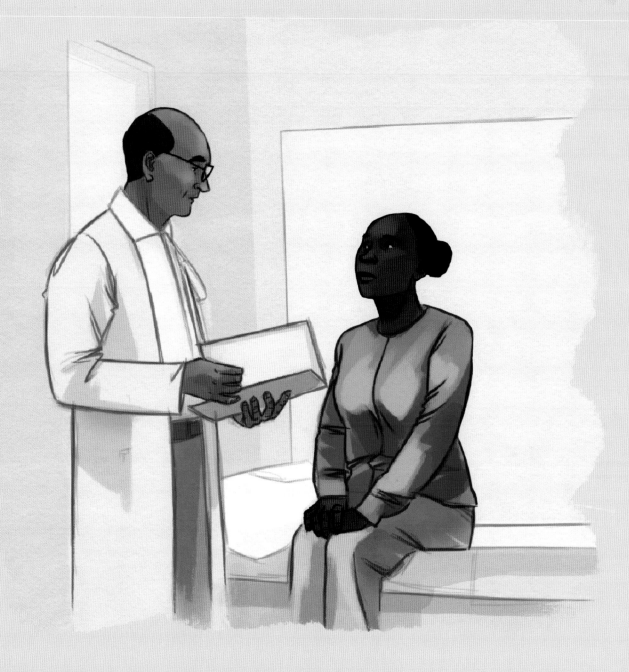

To make matters worse, the doctors gave Venus a difficult diagnosis. She had Sjögren's syndrome, a disease that sometimes made her too exhausted to get out of bed, let alone play tennis.

Venus and Serena thought about walking away from tennis for good.

They'd already accomplished the unimaginable, like becoming the first sisters ever to be ranked number one and number two in the world. They'd already made their family proud, by standing up against racism and for women's equality.

What was the point of playing tennis anymore?

Maybe this was the end of their story.

But then they asked themselves, "What would Yetunde want?"

Deep down, Venus and Serena knew that they weren't done yet.

The Williams sisters still had work to do.

So the sisters slowly picked each other back up.

Venus cheered for Serena at all her matches. Whenever she was losing, Venus cheered even harder.

Soon, Serena was playing better than ever. Her ranking had fallen to 139 by 2006 . . . but in 2008 she was back at number one. Even when her ranking fell from the top spot, Serena was the undisputed best player in the world.

Serena stayed by her big sister's side as Venus battled Sjögren's.

When Venus was too tired to leave the house, Serena squeezed

her hand and said, "Don't you dare give up!"

Soon, Venus felt strong enough to return to the court. And not

just to return—but to win.

The sisters were once again at the peak
of the tennis world.

They dominated the biggest tournaments,
won Olympic gold medals, and soared to the top
of the rankings.

And when they teamed up to play doubles,
they were truly unstoppable.

Both women were in their thirties, an age when most tennis players retire.

But the fire that began when they were children only grew stronger, and they played harder than ever.

Throughout their careers, Venus and Serena thought about the place where their tennis careers had begun.

In 2016, they returned to their crumbling courts in Compton.

And they fixed all the cracks.

They opened tennis camps, organized tennis clinics, and hired the best coaches in California to teach kids how to love tennis as much as they did.

Today, those courts are called the Venus and Serena Williams Court of Champions.

At the grand opening of the Court of Champions, Venus and Serena couldn't stop grinning. They watched siblings pick up racquets for the first time. They watched families heal.

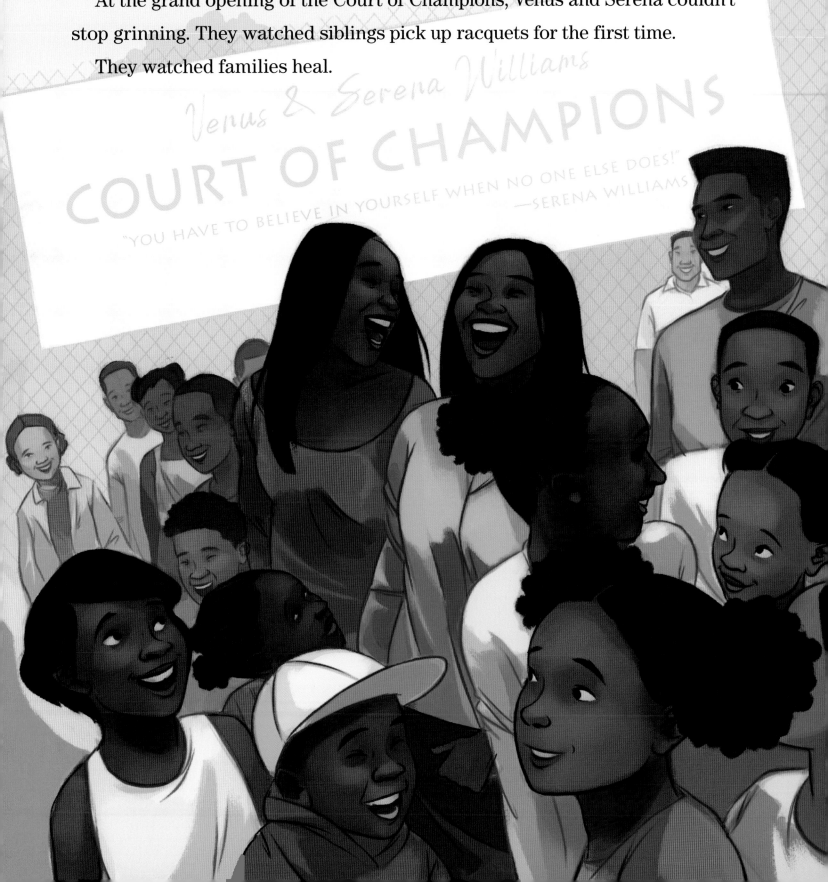

The sisters also founded the Yetunde Price Resource Center to help victims of violence.

No one should ever lose a sister the way they'd lost Yetunde.

To this day, Serena keeps a trophy on her bedside table.
It's more precious than Olympic gold or any Grand Slam
championship cup.

It's the trophy that Venus gave her after their first tournament.
Serena looks at it every night before she goes to sleep, because it
reminds her of one very important thing:

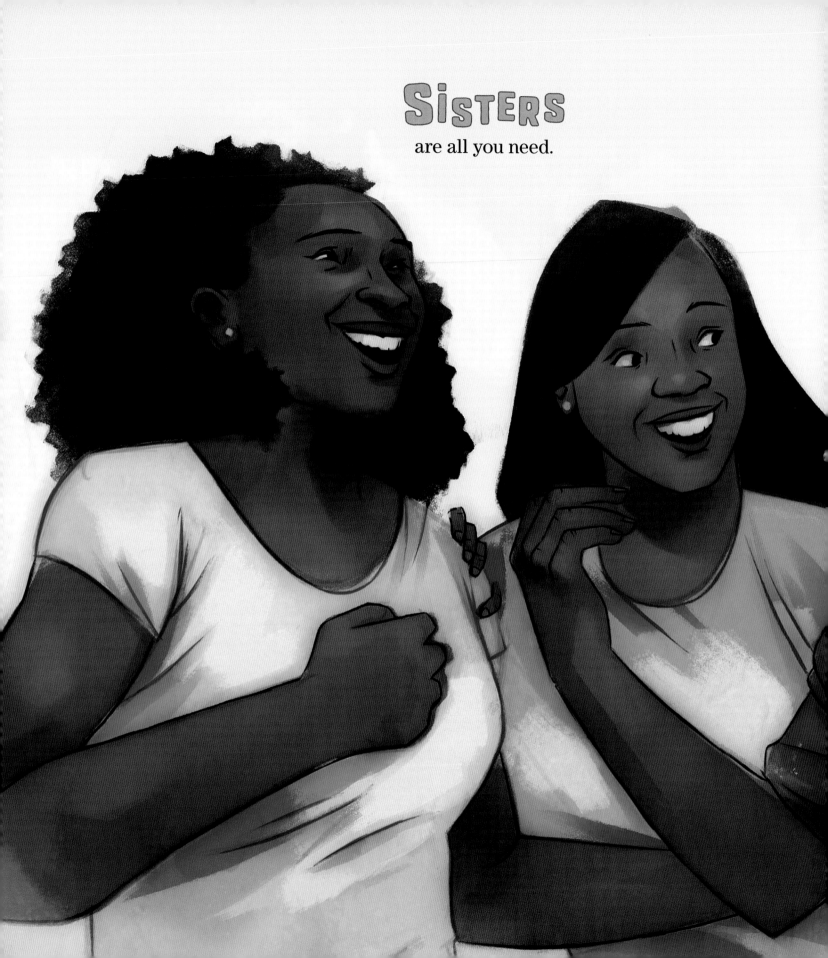

Sisters

are all you need.

TIME LINE

1980: Venus Williams is born on June 17.

1981: Serena Williams is born on September 26.

1989: Venus and Serena face each other in a tournament for the first time.

1991: Venus and Serena move to Florida to attend the Rick Macci Tennis Academy.

1994: Venus turns pro.

1995: Serena turns pro.

1999: Serena wins the US Open in September, becoming the first Williams sister to obtain a Grand Slam title.

2000: Venus wins her first Grand Slam singles title at Wimbledon, followed by her second Grand Slam title at the US Open and the singles gold medal at the Olympic Games in Sydney, Australia. The sisters win the gold medal in doubles, too.

2001: The crowd jeers both sisters during the Indian Wells tournament in May. Venus and Serena agree to boycott the event.

2002: Venus rises to the top of the world rankings for the first time in February. That year, after the French Open in June, Venus is ranked number one and Serena is ranked number two, marking the first time in history that sisters hold the top two spots. Serena becomes world number one in July.

2003: Serena wins the Australian Open in January, her fourth Grand Slam title in a row, after winning the French Open, Wimbledon, and the US Open the previous year. She calls her victory the "Serena Slam."

2003: Later that same year, in September, Serena and Venus's sister Yetunde Price is killed in Compton.

2006: In April, Serena's ranking falls out of the top 100 for the first time since 1997.

2007: Venus's fight for gender equality leads to equal pay for women and men for the first time at Wimbledon.

2011: Venus is diagnosed with Sjögren's syndrome.

2012: Venus and Serena become the first doubles team to win Olympic gold medals three times.

2015: In March, Serena plays the BNP Paribas Open in Indian Wells for the first time since 2001. She reaches the semifinals.

2016: Venus returns to the BNP Paribas Open in Indian Wells in March. She loses in the second round.

2016: The same year, in November, Venus and Serena found the Yetunde Price Resource Center and open the Venus and Serena Williams Court of Champions.

2017: Venus makes it to the finals of the Australian Open and Wimbledon. Serena defeats her sister in Australia, marking her twenty-third Grand Slam singles title. That September, she gives birth to her first child.

SELECTED SOURCES

Baird, Maiken, and Michelle Major, directors. *Venus and Serena*. New York: Magnolia Pictures, 2013. Retrieved from http://magpictures.com/venusandserena.

Friedman, Lauren F., and Rebecca Harrington. "The Story Behind Venus Williams' Off-Court Struggle." Business Insider. September 8, 2015. https://businessinsider.com/venus-williams-fight-against-sjogrens-syndrome-2015-9.

Harris, Beth. "Straight Back to Compton: Venus and Serena Williams Go Home." AP News. November 12, 2016. https://apnews.com/2528beeb20cc47f1837a7e55c3727a53/Straight-back-to-Compton:-Venus-and-Serena-Williams-go-home.

Roenigk, Alyssa. "Road to 23: The Story of Serena's Path to Greatness." ESPN.com. Updated March 27, 2020. https://www.espn.com/espnw/culture/feature/story/_/id/17494146/road-23-story-serena-path-greatness.

Williams, Serena, with Daniel Paisner. *On the Line*. New York: Grand Central Publishing, 2009.

Yetunde Price Resource Center, A Williams Sisters Project Fund. https://yprcla.org.

ADDITIONAL READING

Bryant, Howard. *Sisters and Champions: The True Story of Venus and Serena Williams*. New York: Philomel Books, 2018.

Cline-Ransome, Lesa. *Game Changers: The Story of Venus and Serena Williams*. New York: Paula Wiseman Books, 2018.

Wetzel, Dan. *Epic Athletes: Serena Williams*. New York: Henry Holt and Company, 2019.

In memory of my tennis coach, Coach Kofi Mawougbe,
who taught me that tennis is a lifelong sport. "Move your feet!"
—J. L.

For Serena, Venus, Isha, Yetunde, and Lyndrea.
—E. G.

Henry Holt and Company, *Publishers since 1866*
Henry Holt® is a registered trademark of Macmillan Publishing Group, LLC
120 Broadway, New York, NY 10271
mackids.com

Text copyright © 2021 by Jamie McGhee
Illustrations copyright © 2021 by Ebony Glenn

Library of Congress Cataloging-in-Publication Data
Names: Leslie, Jay, author. | Glenn, Ebony, illustrator.
Title: Game, set, sisters! : the story of Venus and Serena Williams / Jay Leslie ; illustrated by Ebony Glenn.
Description: First edition. | New York : Henry Holt and Company, 2021. | Series: Who did it first? |
Includes bibliographical references. | Audience: Ages 4–8. | Audience: Grades 2–3. | Summary: "An uplifting picture book biography
about the unwavering bond between sisters and tennis legends Venus and Serena Williams" —Provided by publisher.
Identifiers: LCCN 2020021759 | ISBN 9781250307408 (hardcover)
Subjects: LCSH: Williams, Venus, 1980– —Juvenile literature. | Williams, Serena, 1981– —Juvenile literature. | Tennis players—
United States—Biography—Juvenile literature. | African American women tennis players—Biography—Juvenile literature. |
Sisters—United States—Biography—Juvenile literature.
Classification: LCC GV994.W49 L47 2021 | DDC 796.342092/52—dc23
LC record available at https://lccn.loc.gov/2020021759

Our books may be purchased in bulk for promotional, educational, or business use.
Please contact your local bookseller or the Macmillan Corporate and Premium Sales Department at
(800) 221-7945 ext. 5442 or by email at MacmillanSpecialMarkets@macmillan.com.

First edition, 2021 / Designed by Angela Jun
The artist used Adobe Photoshop to create the art for this book.
Printed in China by RR Donnelley Asia Printing Solutions Ltd., Dongguan City, Guangdong Province

1 3 5 7 9 10 8 6 4 2